Praise for *CHILDREN, IT IS TIME WE HAD THE TALK*

This collection is a wild ride of wicked, surreal fun, like Mary Poppins dispensing wisdom while on a whole lot of pills. Whether you're a mother, or have a mother, or are simply alive in these strange times, trying to cling to the bright life raft of the imagination, you need these poems. A spoonful of Maddalena's poetry helps the medicine go down.

— Mindy Nettifee, author of *Sleepyhead Assassins*, *Rise of the Trust Fall*, and *Glitter in the Blood*

Cheryl Maddalena's new collection *CHILDREN, IT IS TIME WE HAD THE TALK* is a brilliant tangle of joy and shame, magic and mundane, hilarious and haunting. Maddalena confronts with rug-pulling honesty the sometimes queasy ambivalence of being a mother, a woman, many women, sometimes Marilyn Monroe, sometimes a chainsaw juggler, and still and always a child herself. With a quick-moving kind of magic realism, the poet here is determined to jet-pack her way toward a world she can barely see on the horizon, one where we all are no longer governed by the whip of our own expectations.

—Doc Luben, author of *Love Letters Or Suicide Notes*, co-artistic director of Portland Poetry Slam

CHILDREN, IT IS TIME WE HAD THE TALK

poems by
Cheryl Maddalena

BLUE SKETCH PRESS | PITTSBURGH

CHILDREN, IT IS TIME WE HAD THE TALK. Copyright © 2017 by Cheryl Maddalena.
All rights reserved by author including right of reproduction in whole or in part or in any form. For information, address Blue Sketch Press, 1124 De Victor Pl., Pittsburgh, PA 15206.

Please see "Acknowledgments" page for acknowledgments of previous publication.

www.bluesketchpress.com
www.facebook.com/bluesketchpress.com

Children, It Is Time We Had The Talk
by Cheryl Maddalena — 1st ed.
      ISBN (print)   978-1-942547-07-5 (trade paperback)

Illustrations by Sarah Rachel
Cover & Interior Design by Little Owl Creative
Edited by Joseph N. Welch, III.

First Edition: August 2017

Printed in the United States of America
9 8 7 6 5 4 3 2 1

For my family, who I hope will never read this.

CONTENTS

Part 1: FOUNDATIONS

Housewife	13
Marilyn	17
Second to the Left	20
Medusa Brings Her Sons to Chuck E. Cheese	21
The Dissociator's Switch	24
Heimlich	26

Part 2: ROOMS

The Talk	33
Redneck Safari / Sunroofs for Giraffes	35
Dear White Boys	39
Polite Invitation	41
Boys and Guns	43
Reception	46
Embalming	47
The Reasons	51

Part 3: THINGS TO DO

The Visit	54
An Appointment	57
Chad Vargo	58
Wonder Woman, Princess Leia, and Buffy the Vampire Slayer Have Tea	60
Cesarean	64
Hobby	68
The 10 A.M. YMCA Dance Class	69
Acknowledgments	75
About the Author	77

Part 1:
FOUNDATIONS

HOUSEWIFE

When I realized I was married
to... my... house...

I glued dildos to every seat
wrote love notes to the toaster
took steamy showers with
the shower.
We were newlyweds
batteries fresh
toast hot
the soap scum of infidelities
with the soap
impossible.
The way my hand caressed
the long, thick banister
everyone knew
we were
in love.

I read Housemopolitan magazines for tips
on how to intimately please it.
Bought special brushes
for the toilet.
Coordinated my clothes with the curtains

so people would say how
CUTE
we were
while they were standing
out on our doorstep
because the dildos
made them
afraid.

Or did they?
Was my washing machine's round front-loading eye
avoiding my gaze? Gas burners seemed
to flicker blue secrets. I became
suspicious. Was my home
a ho?
Mmm?

So I sold our minivan and bought a baby blue Vespa
with Hello Kitty decals on it.
Trashed my pink cashmere pearl-button sweater set
and got some thigh-high boots and a miniskirt
that totally clashed
with our carpet.
People were all, "You're married to a house?!"
And I was all, "Yeah, like, I know, I look way
too sex-ay for that! I totally look, you know,
like I'm dating an
apartment."

When I got home looking all wind-tossed and fetching
things had gone wonky. The front porch light
was blinky. The microwave was ionizing
fondue forks. Lamps were
fast-rubbing blisters

on the wall.
The refrigerator eased down the hall skimming sustenance through
its icemaker
spitting cubes filled with teeth
and hair.
The stove beat its chest in frustration.
It was really fucking scary!

Tradition dictated a fifty-thousand dollar
kitchen makeover
and Viagra.
Convention insisted on any solution that was expensive and
boring.
The open maw of the basement was roaring,
"Shove money in me!"

How did it come to this?
I knew sometimes women and abodes grew apart
but I never thought it would happen
to us.
I thought about the time I brought home
our first Kitchen-Aid stand mixer
and we made brownies
from scratch
and they came out too gooey
but we decided we would
always make them
like that.

The beer bottles were flopping upstairs to die.
It was time to decide. Walls were oozing
spaghetti sauce and lube.
Our multicolored flock of dildos was trembling
with rage from the safety of a bathtub

filled with Perrier and velvet
accent cushions.

"Stop!" I shouted. "I'm sorry! You are
the kinky mansion of my dreams
and desires!"
The appliances all fell quiet. I closed my eyes
and when I opened them
all that was left
of the residinsanity was a note scrawled over the bed:

"Don't replace your sweater set."

MARILYN

I dreamed I was Marilyn Monroe, and I kissed me.
    I was so surprised.
I said, "Marilyn honey, I thought we were dead!"

"It is so wonderful to see us," I chimed in.
    "I missed us so much."
I took my face in my hands and looked so deep
    into my eyes I had to look away.
"Woah. Okay."

"Let's get dressed and go get breakfast?" I suggested.
    "Yes," I agreed.
"But I just have to say I am such a wonderful sight.
    Nothing's been the same without me, Marilyn."

We got dressed. I wore blue, I wore red, and I kissed
    me again
because I could, because I was beautiful, because I'd
    missed me so much.
I was blonde, I was brown, fifteen and thirty-five
    and smiling like sunrises
except in my eyes. We went to a 50's themed diner,
    pretending not to see
the grubby pierced teenagers staring at me,

at me, at us.
Eating buttered toast, eggs, black coffee and bacon
    a short stack of pancakes
smeared with grape jam, while under the table
    I kept squeezing
my adorable knee. I simply couldn't keep my hands
    off me.
Couldn't stop smiling sunrises at me and I was used
    to the part
about the sadness in my eyes. I didn't even care
    it was so good
to see me, to see us alive again, after all of the
    wondering, the searching
and lies. The answers all trapped in loose white
    purgatory.

It had been awful without me

and as we got up to leave I took my hand tightly like I
    might never let go again.
I was kind of hurting me but we understood
    what we meant.
We understood that Norma Jeane Marilyn sometimes
    needed to hold so tightly
because we could feel the world spinning,
    and the abyss
was filled with purgatory and we could hear the
    silence like screaming,
and no matter how much beauty we shined we could
    never lose the taste of nothingness.

I held my hand even more tightly as we strolled
    down the street
like bosom buddies with the most famous bosom

in the world.
It was like old times, imaginary times really,
    when we had time
for a day to just be a girl, feeling the sun warm on
    our glowing skin.
"If only it could always be like this," I said to the
    me in red,
and I could not believe what I had just heard us say.
    "Dammit!" I hissed.
"These bonds can only bring me grief with men,
    and now this?
Not just a woman but my very own self? How many
    times must I say it?
I see inside. I know what we hide and I refuse to
    ever face it.
Not for us, not for anyone! And I may be somewhat
    lesbian,
but we are not my type."

The sun was still bright on the sidewalk but we were
    trembling blue and red
and I shook me, screaming, "It was just breakfast!"
    But I wrenched
away, running down the street in high heels, until…
staring at my beautiful back until… until…

Until I woke up.
I kind of stumbled to the bathroom, flipped on the
    light and squinted
at my pale, greasy, bed-headed, funky-breathed
    reflection.
And then I kissed me.

SECOND TO THE LEFT

You think you'll
make the alcoholic not drink,
fill the hole shaped
like an absent Madonna,
lure the workaholic to
happyfuntime.

Don't you wonder why
you hold the role of catalyst,
the tendon, the phone line,
the crying pillow? Are
you an executive assistant?
Vice President? Fourth
wife?

MEDUSA BRINGS HER SONS TO CHUCK E. CHEESE

While the children play with toys of violence
she glides to the malevolent shower
turns on the blood
hums Christmas carols under her breath
baritone.
The snakes accompany with their contralto.
She brushes one hundred thirty two teeth
smooths skin with Neutrogena
throws fifty white mice in the air
her secret styling trick
to tame unruly locks.

Panties and push up bra
(you need all the help you can get
when you're over two thousand)
a deep blue dress with a plunging neckline
and flat shoes for endurance.
Fifty reedy voices protest
as pincurl snakes are tucked
under a Marilyn wig.
The silver of her eyes
is hidden under colored contacts
aqua for the sea, for impossible colors
aqua for everything impossible.

Before she calls out,
"Children, in the car! Seatbelts!"
she pushes the barbed spears of her voice
through a thousand banks of violets.
In the rearview she sees those boys
smooth cheeks bright and curving
like the Earth seen from the palace of the Gods.
She doesn't remember how she got them.
Probably stole them or ate their parents.
But after thousands of years
to always and only rage seemed silly.
Seemed an echo, only echoing itself.

Still, the purple-belted warehouse
takes an inhuman, mighty strength to enter.
As the wheels and bells and squeals and lights
and vague sticky substrates
swallow her and the boys
she clutches the stone that is her heart.
Remembers, she's been beheaded
and she got through that just fine.
The time for trying to understand is behind
and in front, twin planets, hands held out.
Forgive how her wig roils in protest
at the unreachable, uneatable mouse.

THE DISSOCIATOR'S SWITCH

Things that are not good for the dissociator:

1. Fucking Around.
The spirit sits cross-legged
in the far corner of the ceiling
eating a big bag of popcorn and
noticing how freakishly unsymmetrical
people are up close.
Weird.

2. Monotheistic Religions.
Prayer is an archaic catapult
throwing the spirit at a target in the sky.
Like how a boy in junior high flips pencils up
end over end over end over end
at the round holes in
asbestos ceilings.

3. Arguing.
"Well, I don't see it
that way. The way I see it is...
...Faack, I'm on the far side of Saturn.
It's pretty here. So. Pretty.
Whoa."

*4. Bowls Of Melted Butter
Accidentally Poured In Lap By Waitress.*
Really.

Things that are good for the dissociator:

*Flowers.
Faces.
Fireflies.*

HEIMLICH

I finally got so lonely
I started making myself choke
so people would Heimlich me.

For an instant
a single shrimp
soaring from my glottal stop *
it's like I matter.

Took a long time to figure out
how to make people care about me.
When I was four
I was the best color
in the rainbow ballet—purple.
Everyone clapped.
But that night, when I brushed my teeth
no one clapped then.

So I tried harder.
Got an A in cursive writing.
Made a Mount Rushmore sculpture
of the four assassinated presidents
at the moments of their deaths.
  :0   :0   :0   :0

Became hula hoop champion of New Orleans.
But praise was fleeting.

I tried harder.
Took college level physics.
Learned to square dance.
Developed bulimia so pulchritudinous
I could do tricks.
There are pictures:
Me, in a silver-spangled leotard
juggling chainsaws, on a tightrope
spouting a perfect arc
of semi-digested something
into a tiny tin bucket
held by a monkey in suspenders.

Once this kid in my class got cancer.
It was terrible.
Until he finally! died.

I think about death sometimes.
I know a guy who reads obituaries
because he's happy for people.
I know a girl
who pulls her truck
into the processional behind hearses.

I know a horse
who dreams of glue.
nicker

Some say life is about service
or work, or love
but what if that's just convenient

because they already like that stuff?

What if our achievements merely
smother unpleasant feelings?
That Eiffel Tower architect:
So needy.
Bill and Melinda Gates:
Overcompensates.

But the pursuit of only pleasure
is a Ferris wheel it costs a lot to ride.
And the pleasure of pursuing goals
is a rollercoaster shiny loop de loop
where you have to be Sisyphus
and the rock.
Rolling yourself through
goal after goal after goal after goal
after goal—forever.

But sometimes
I imagine the people trudging by me
as brave, bold, and beaming.
No matter who they are
I know how they would be like.

And when I am lonely
I pretend that I am choking.
Even a stranger
will put their arms around you
when they know
it will save
your life.

Part 2:
ROOMS

THE TALK

Children, it is time
we had the sex talk.
First, always be careful
with your elbows.
They can leave a mark.

Every time you have sex
you will make a baby.
The good babies will fend
for themselves:
find their own homes
in your sleeping armpits
in your drawers
curling up kittenish
in the shining circles of your pores.
The medium-good babies
will still blend in with the décor.
And the others,
well now you know
what's been gunking up the wheels
on the carts in grocery stores.
When you find yourself always listing left
scraping and bumping along every aisle
now you know why now.

Someday, children,
sex will be so old hat
you'll fall asleep while you're doing it.

The last thing you need to know
is about condoms.
Some of them are cherry flavor
and some glow in the dark.
Be sure every time you have sex
to unroll one over your heart.

REDNECK SAFARI / SUNROOFS FOR GIRAFFES

The most awesome moments in life
answer questions
you would never think to ask.
So when you buy a minivan
make sure to get a sunroof
for the giraffes.
Your minivan will be
juice-cracker-candy-glue-glitter-burger-booger encrusted,
and will have a bad smell you cannot find.
And you will not like the bad smell
and you will remember wearing
clean clothes and self esteem.
Life can be so humbling
that you forget how to dream.

But then we were visiting friends
in North Carolina for Christmas
and they said,
"We have to go to Lazy Five Ranch.
It's the Redneck Safari."
So in the front were the two dads
who used to ski with beers in their jackets
and the two moms were in the back
with their unused doctorates.

And rattling around
the middle of the minivan
where we pulled out the seats
were our combined five boys
ages 2, 3, 4, 5, and 6
all holding big buckets
of Wild Animal Chow
so that seven hundred wild
(presumably herbivorous) animals
could mob our minivan
stick their heads in our windows
and eat the chow
from our beautiful babies' buckets of it.

A flock of emu
six feet tall and ostrichey
eyes crazy wide and blue
jet pistoned triangular beaks down
centimeters from my baby's face
to spray chow to the ceiling of the minivan.
The boys were all screaming
like they'd been mass electrocuted
with excitement.

There were gazelles,
dark hairy potbellied pigs,
a lot of things I couldn't name,
and zebras.
A buffalo's gruesomely enormous head
entered the front passenger window
to run its thick grey tongue
along the inside towards the handle.
It was a little scary.
I'm not even a dog person.

The kids were live squealing pinballs
ricocheting and roaring
as we drove slowly along.
The dads laughing and smiling
like good dogs out on a run.
The moms
two cans of anxiety soup
with "stress is good food" on the labels—
and then, there we were
paused at the top of a clearing
offering our buckets out the sunroof
to the gold and brown
puzzle piece face of a giraffe.
A giraffe!
All long lashes and fuzzy horns
and a really fierce and smelly drool
that dripped down to the gear shift.
A giraffe,
a real giraffe
right in the minivan's sunroof.

Until that moment
I never knew
how much I wanted that to happen.
Those five shrieking kids
caroming around a sticky minivan
spraying animal chow
like unfortunate manna.
Dodging giraffe drool in North Carolina.
Just when you think
nothing new will ever happen again.
The most awesome things in life
are the ones you couldn't plan.

DEAR WHITE BOYS

Dear white boys,
I love how you glow
    in the dark.
Your freckles
    are reverse constellations
    always Orion, and Elvis.
    Orion, and Elvis.

At three a.m.
    I can see you matching moonlight
    as you stride down dingy apartment hallways
    toward me.
The negative space of the curves of your face
    are woodblock prints against the ceiling.
Even with the lights out
    the streetlamps
    clock diodes
    your blinking iPhone charger
    the reflections from your waterglass
illuminate you in my arms.

Your cock
    is a Lite Brite peg
    grown to your genetic code.

Your nipples float above me
        like dark cherries
        à la mode.

This is why I always lie
        when you ask me what I'm thinking.
I'm watching you flush pink.
You are a blank tablet begging ink.
The curve of your shoulder so luminous
        I forget how to think.

I am watching the moon rise, alone.
I am watching stars reflect off the ocean.
My hands
        trace the outline of a phantom.
No wonder I invite you in.

POLITE INVITATION

I am cooking the salsa of hate.
Hot stove, capsaicin
        embedded into the pores of my palms,
six onions
        chopped by the engine of my resentment,
a laundry basket full of tomatoes
        with flesh pulled so tight
they are as near to bursting as my temper.

Come to dinner.

I will set the table
        as we make the small talk of our kind.
Fill your water glass
        as we say what good workers Mexicans are.
Here is your napkin,
        shudder with pleasure that we avoided downtown
        the day of the gay pride parade this year,
can you imagine?

My shish kebabs
        are all stabbing voodoo dolls of you
        made of vegetables.
Zucchini you, mushroom cap you.

Yellow pepper you to stab your heart.
I am making the potato salad
       of ineffective responses.
It's just potatoes and mayo.
I don't wonder at Molotov barbeques.

BOYS AND GUNS

I have a round headed boy with a beaming daisy face,
and I love him like tectonic plates. He's
on our front steps, brandishing his
lightsaber at a new playdate
and before that little boy
is halfway to the door
he crows,

"You need a weapon.
I will get you one."

Before there were guns, boys made sticks
into swords. Before there were swords,
boys made sticks into…
sticks.

I was never going to buy my children weapons.

So they made guns of cars, guns of wood,
guns of bent Barbie dolls and toast.
Swords of the cardboard rolls
from wrapping paper.
Invisible swords.

They say, "Let's wrestle. Let's box."
Dropping five year olds to the ground like:
Castles of blocks.
Dirty socks.
Chicken pox.

"Let's have a war! You're Iraq! I'm the Sith!
Come with us to rescue the baby giraffe's neck.
These pillows are our bombs.
These pillows are our fort.
These pillows are the
cozy bed in our fort.
I'm Batman.
You're Sharkboy.
Boom! Boom!"

My children were never going to eat corn dogs
and watch old cartoons until their potential
smurfed away like smurfy dreams.
My children were going to eat okra
and speak Cantonese.
And my boys

were going to play with little pink dollies,
not lightsabers that glow
Batman swords that clang
and Nerf ball guns
with ammo
that doesn't
even hurt
when you
get shot
in the
face.

But little boys are warriors, and weapons
are their medium for cooperation
sharing, and the earsplitting love
screeching out from the mighty
bottoms of their
savage lungs.

"Please kill each other very gently," I say.
"Are you sure you're all having fun?"
A battalion of bright heads pauses
to nod and smile at me.
Boys will use branches
fat with pink buds
for guns:
Bloom.
Bloom.

RECEPTION

When I bring you a damn crocus
a currently shooting star
the crown of my steaming baby's head
pushing impossibly through my vagina

please stop telling me
how I've always been. That this
is exactly what is expected.
I'm not asking for confetti bursts

every time my heart beats.
I know spring comes each year. But
I brought you the crocus for
love, my dear

EMBALMING

A psychiatric illness leading to unreasonable expectations for the surgical outcome, such as a distorted perception of reality, can be a contraindication for surgery.

When my parents visited me and the children
they encouraged, "Get your face lift early!
Why wait?"

I marinated on their well-meaning wisdom
in a Jacuzzi tub of salt, oil, and perfume
for seventy days and sixty-nine nights.
Maybe they were right.

And if so,
I needed more than a facelift alone.
I either had some age spots or chocolate fever.
My eyes scrinkled a little
when I smiled into the faces of my friends.
And god knows no one could love me
if I wasn't fucking
fantabulous.

So I skipped straight to embalming.

Mercury, antimony, Twinkies,
polysorbate 60 and linen strips.
I did it all.
No rotting putrescence
for this corpse body, not me.

Palpate my cadaver.
I am Tutankhamun without the clubfoot.

Rigor mortis keeps me firm.
Cloves, cinnamon, myrrh,
just a touch of ambergris
where my aspirated innards used to been.
I have halted life's decomposition.
A glorious sarcophagus of a woman.
Gotdamn, gotdamn.

And I am so much happier.
My friends say,
"You look so good I could kill you!"
As we play mahjong,
rattling a cup of my finger bones
drinking gasoline martinis
and complaining how the maids
knocked my tits askew when they dusted again.

The transition was difficult,
but beauty is pain.

The full body cavity incision on my left
was not a game.
But the evisceration of my entrails
gave me the concave hollow stomach
I've always craved.

And the rosemary string they sewed me with?
Trust: This bitch is trussed.

The children can bring "Mummy" to school for Show and Tell.
And my parents? Well now they're just jealous.

It can be inconvenient.
The dog made off with my femur
more than once.
But my husband says the sex
has never been better.
My patellas on his earlobes
clacking and knocking
make him come so hard
it leaks out my eye sockets.

The jugular drainage of my arterial blood
was cathartic as a fresh round of weeping.
Circulatory clots sucked through a hypodermic:
a reverse eight ball coursing through my skin.
And I can't lie.
I've added some resin.

I woke up like this.
Archaeologists dig me up like this.
I will always be just like this

for I shall never change nor age again.

THE REASONS

Because my mother kept telling me I wasn't a
Real virgin with all the (disgusting) things I'd done,
Or we were going to get married anyway, or I
Called Bud and he said Brian had finally used a
Condom so I was the last one, the very last
One. When I finally left him about a year
Later, he said, "You stole my virginity. And
I ate broccoli for you."

Part 3:
THINGS TO DO

THE VISIT

The cement walkway to Uncle Al Pelletier's house
is lined with bright marigolds, which are singing.
My heart is a giant hug approaching the screen door.
There's a delighted
"Cheryl Jean! We didn't expect you!"
and I am swept into the tiny kitchen
by my lovely Aunt Lil.

She's Grace Kelly slim in white pants and trim shirt,
skin rose petal sweet as my cheek presses her neck.
I don't want to let go but I do.
Aunt Lil says, "Hey kiddo, go find Albert,"
and the kitchen is filled with doves cooing
on the table, on the stepstool in the corner,
on the cool cans of 7 UP in the refrigerator,

but I am in the living room
on the knobbly white couch with my little brother, who is two, and
I am four.
Uncle Al crouches before us, bright blue eyes beaming. "Watch this,
Cheryl Jean, this is magic."
He rolls the fan of his fingers to the right
and to the left again saying, "No-Shnuf-Num-Pop" with each
repetition and my uncle IS magic.

I can tell
because a bright parrot emerges from his fingers
and squawks, "Have a beer, Pelletier!" We both laugh
because he had that bird years before I was born.
My brother is playing on the keys of Aunt Lil's organ
and between the soft clicks and low notes
I hear my grandfather's voice intone, "Albert
isn't good at coping."
Which surprises me. I always forget they are brothers.

I get up to use the pink and black tiled bathroom
but there is a World War II warship on fire
in the sink.
Tiny men are jumping off it into the ocean
but the ocean is on fire, fuel spilled and ignited
and my Uncle, just nineteen in the flaming water
is screaming, "Lilian dies! Lilian dies!"

I scream too and run back to the living room
where I have pink hair and am 29.
My mother and I sit on the worn white couch
with tears in our eyes
as Uncle Al holds Aunt Lil's weak and shaking hands and says,
"I take good care of her, she's my girl."
Her hair is cropped short and she needs help
to walk. "Isn't she beautiful," he says.

Behind me in the spare bedroom I'm four years old
jumping on the guest bed in my yellow
summer pajamas. The air is filled
with suspended portraits of Aunt Lil, all sizes,
twisting softly in a wind I cannot feel. Uncle Al says, "This is how I
decorated my apartment after."

As I turn to him
I see his bedroom door is closed.

When I put my palm to it, I feel so afraid.
I can hear his ragged breathing behind it
and a sudden sound I don't like and the door
is the last Christmas card I ever got from him.
I'm so afraid but I open it anyway.
The inscription "with love" has been unwritten.

That's it.
He has undone his life with a gun.
No one knows why he did it.
      He is gone.

My uncle stands beside me, his arm, still good
and strong around my shoulders.
"Don't think about that, Cheryl Jean,"
he says. "That was just the last moment."

AN APPOINTMENT

Lie still. Don't
move. Don't think
of your children
or the sun.

There is a pinch
and a burn
and then the far away
tugging.

Don't think of the
awful. Of the
cut. Of the
pieces you'll lose.

It's just a
biopsy, just a sample.
You'll lose all
the pieces in the end.

CHAD VARGO

To the adults who believe that their Innocent Junior High Crushes are, in fact, innocent, I submit this Actual Junior High Memory found stored inside my copy of Shakespeare's Henry IV, required reading for my ninth grade English Insight class.
Ahem:

CHAD VARGO CHAD VARGO
CHAD VARGO CHAD VARGO
I wish you and all the other boys in this class
were licking me right now CHAD VARGO
Your raven locks are well beseeming
I wish you would kiss me for the nonce
Last year we slow-danced, you rogue, you rascal
Now I am wrung in the withers and all out of cess

CHAD VARGO CHAD VARGO
CHAD VARGO CHAD VARGO
Your ill-sheathed knife dost baffle me
Your white high tops are gallantly huge CHAD VARGO
God-a-mercy, what valiance betwixt thy thighs
what scourge of villainous greatness bears hard
in the chair right behind me?
Points it hitherwards, towards me? S'blood! I prithee!

CHAD VARGO CHAD VARGO
CHAD VARGO CHAD VARGO
I am nettled, I'm revolted in a place I cannot name
This naked shore, I daren't even look at it CHAD VARGO
For I want to be with Christ, who is on the cross…
mostly naked, oh Jesus, he does look pretty hot
I'm a necrophiliac blasphemer and I'm going to hell

CHAD VARGO
My skimble skamble stuff is fat as butter in good sooth
I would givest thou a blow job
but I know not how to doeth it
Is it blow, unruly wind? Blow, exhal'd meteor?
And the tongue a helpful ornament? I don't know
I don't know, I am insensible and vex'd

Oh CHAD VARGO, remember how you danced with me?
Hurly burly topsy turvy, is it true you didn't care?
Because I wish you and all the boys in this classroom
were licking me right now, CHAD VARGO
And Jesus too, a candy deal, I'm going to hell and this class is really boring
but I love you CHAD VARGO, zounds! anon, anon! holla!

WONDER WOMAN, PRINCESS LEIA, AND BUFFY THE VAMPIRE SLAYER HAVE TEA

luxurious black locks
twist softly down Amazonian shoulders
as she leans toward you,
gold-shielded cleavage warm
within inches of your trembling mouth.
you are bound and bound to answer
as luscious red lips part to whisper:
"*tell me the truth.*"

oh the wonder! of jungle-grown Diana,
invisible jets of heat steam all
whom she meets, from golden tiara
to red leather booted feet
Wonder Woman, you are hot.
I can't lie to you.
but I see your sign language
as you deflect bullets with silver bracelets
replay the tape back in slow motion:
"someone help me, I am lonely
and need friends and chocolate."

enter Leia Organa
hijacking the Millennium Falcon
two mega parsecs and a time travel boost

and bounding down a banging metal ramp
in her orange jumpsuit:
"Diana, I have received your message
through mental radio and the Force."
at that same moment
a green flash of light blinds the sky
and boom
with a roundhouse kick
bearing a plate of big chocolate bunnies
is blonde Buffy Summers:
"hi."

three heroines stare in silence.
the Millennium Falcon clunkily hovers.
chocolate rabbits listen, ears erect.
"it's hard, being a superhero,"
Wonder Woman finally offers.
"you're never supposed to ask for help."

tears fill her violet-blue eyes
and as each shiny sphere falls
the world is reflected upside down within.
an endless stream of dreary action sequences
replaying over and again
and with each repetition another begins.
as inexorable as laundry
as inevitable as dirty dishes,
as women's work always is.

Diana accepts a chunk of chocolate from Buffy,
tea from Leia's hip flask
and settles her star-spangled booty
in the dusty shadow of the spacecraft.
Leia crouches beside to whisper,

"I can't stay long but I brought you this."
it's a tiny plastic trinket replica
of Han Solo frozen in carbonite.
Buffy hands her a gold locket with pictures
of her dead mother and estranged father inside,
sighs, "it'd be hard even without the vampires."

Diana gratefully smiles.
Leia hugs her
then leaps back into the Falcon
firing up the hyperdrive.
Buffy kisses her forehead
and in a brilliant blonde flash of light
she too is gone.
Wonder Woman, alone
licks her fingers
summons her invisible jet
and in its rearview mirror sternly demands:
"tell me the truth, Diana,
are you happy?"

she thinks of Paradise Island in cascading green,
her love for pilot Steve Trevor.
"am I happy?"
but before she can answer
she hears a distant call for help.
Diana straightens, checks her lipstick.
with the slightest touch of thought
the invisible jet rises into the sky
winking in the sunlight like a shared secret
and Wonder Woman
superheroine
flies to the rescue again.

CESAREAN

legs spread, paralyzed, exhausted and in pain
faceless voices talked of other things
      as over and over again strangers
      had their way with me
but this is not a rape scene
for this people will congratulate me
so I'm supposed to just shut up and be grateful
I got my happy ending
my first child was born a healthy baby

when I planned to deliver my son naturally
people said, "Aren't you scared of the pain?"
I was
but I was even more scared of a cesarean
the impersonal way doctors slice women open
first the skin
then the layer of pale yellow fat
and then the smooth red muscles of the abdomen
      split open like ripe fruit
I was afraid of the burning smell
      from the cauterizing knife
as healthy flesh slits crimson in unnatural dissection

so I just wanted to birth my son vaginally
to hear my husband say, "Oh my God,
        there's his head! You're doing it!"
and I knew an epidural too soon
would ruin my ability to push a head
        through my bones
small women need gravity
        to help their pelvis move open
and I knew that being induced hurts like hell
as luscious budding bloom
        is prematurely plucked and peeled apart
fresh and perfect flesh
        squeezed in a rock hard fist
        until crushed pulp runs to waste

but I was overdue and the doctors threatened me
said, "we can't guarantee your baby's safety"
"we'll just give you something to 'ripen your cervix'"
"this drug will just nudge your natural process"
"yes, it's just like natural labor, we promise"

and so this body was seized in a rictus
        while the doctors safely slept
contractions ten minutes long
        with no breaks
        no time between to say
        "whew, that was a rough one"
just waves upon waves of crushing pain
after hours I begged for relief
I didn't care what would happen

27 hours after the induction
the pain
the anesthetized waiting
      for my 10 centimeter completion
and the two hours of pushing
God!
hearing, "we can see his head"
      "we can see his head"
      "but he's not coming"
I agreed to my cesarean section
signed the form with fingers strange with exhaustion

and then there we were
waiting for the surgery
I might as well have been a dead woman
as strangers wandered through my room
      and made conversation
stared curiously at my shredded crotch
      to heap high humiliation
no, it wasn't a rape scene
so people try to minimize my memory to me
"surely you've forgotten the labor BY NOW"
but when I make love to my husband
      remembered helplessness wells within
I can't help it
being naked just feels different

and I know I'm a woman, it's my lot to endure
so I should just shut up
      and be glad my baby's safety was sure
because deep down
      we believe women are made for abuse
that we should just move on from humiliation
gracefully cope with vile misuse

      with the quiet ease some women seem to

that violation doesn't matter
      if the end result was good
that we should smilingly surrender woman's bloom
      to surgeon's bloody fear
that my body was created
      to become a fragrant ruin
and the only scar that I should carry
      is the one across my womb

HOBBY

I worked all day fitting together a pastoral scene.
I could put your face where the blue sky
is marred by a hole that looks like a man.
Last week my fingers traced the rippling grooves
of a thousand piece mug shot of a fluffy kitten.
There is a space for your cock in her grey eye.
Why else would she look at you like that?

In return I shall shore up your sweet façade.
There are hairline fractures up in your corners.
Your hardwood is dulled, baseboard warping,
the imprint of your angry knuckles embedded
at shoulder height all down the dark hallway.
Smooth my melted substance into your skin.
The ball bearings of your spine click soft again.

When my heart scissors sideways, trapped flat
between carefully constructed cardboard layers,
don't wake me. I am dreaming of growing things.
When your bookshelf spills out leather-bound
earthquakes, when your ice cubes clink restless,
when the sight of mountains twists your face
into ugly shapes, I will pretend not to notice.

THE 10 A.M. YMCA DANCE CLASS

The arching popcorn ceiling squashes down
to peach and blue cinder blocks
depressing as the sound
of my old gym teacher
and Spanish teacher
kissing.

A worn wall of mirrors reflects fifty pale female ovals
hovering over workout camis and yoga pants
with two retired tie-dyed hippie dudes
in white socks and tennis shoes
for flavor.

But when the clock strikes ten everything changes.
It's the 10 AM YMCA dance class.

Now when I was eleven I flunked ballet.
My left ass cheek
is statistically significantly less coordinated than average.
I've been tested. I'm awkward and thin-skinned
and when a band tries to get the audience
to clap in time
I don't bother.

But when I was nine I performed interpretive dance
to both albums of Jesus Christ Superstar
in the dining room just for me.
When I was fourteen I saw Dirty Dancing
and if Baby could land Patrick Swayze
maybe it was okay to dream.
In my twenties
beer bottle in hand
I scanned darkened rooms
for any guy worthwhile to shadow.

A girl's gift is to shadow.
Do everything the man does
backward in heels and he will tell you you're amazing
because you are a reflection of him. A girl is a blank book
to be written in.

I'm a nostalgic woman.
Turn my own pages, read myself
in others' fingerprints like lines on skin.
But after a while
I got tired of reading
"have a nice summer" and "you're a kewl girl"
and hundreds of creamy perfect pages awaited me
are me
all for me.

The miracle
of the 10 AM YMCA dance class
is not the music, which is far better
than the sultry pop synth grind that PYTs endure
in Boise nightly.
It is not even the teacher

in faded workout pants and ball cap
maybe a couple years older than me and still
mighty pretty.
The miracle
is the discovery
of momentum. First the brain
bravely connects the feet to the correct rhythm.
Then the arms. It would be better if they were perfect
but whatever.
Look at the two hippie dudes
they're okay and so are you. Last comes
the arc of the spine and the head. My head
really wants to keep making sure I'm doing it right
so I don't always get there. I don't always get there.

But there are moments
sometimes when 50 gorgeous
humans are literally flying in time to the moment.
When the body opens up
the spirit flows in and I know it.
I know what I want. I know what I am.
And there are times
when my feet aren't working.
I can never look in the mirror because my insides
hiss, "no one could ever love you." I want to slam myself closed and
run.

Over and again
I have to choose
to be nothing or to be a woman.
"Are you going to live your fucking life or not?"
And it's the music that answers:
"I'm living this life like it's golden, golden.

Living this life like it's golden.
I'm living this life like it's golden, golden.
Living this life like it's golden."

ACKNOWLEDGMENTS

"Housewife" was published in the Spring 2014 issue of *Wilderness House Literary Review*.

"Marilyn" was published in the May 2014 issue of *PANK*.

Both are reprinted with permission from the author.

ABOUT THE AUTHOR

Cheryl Maddalena is a poet, mom, engineer, and psychologist... but not all at the same time. Sometime slammaster of Boise, she has reached National Poetry Slam, Individual World Poetry Slam, Group Piece, and Women of the World Poetry Slam Finals stages as a competitor, backup dancer, emcee, and opening act. She has also made top four at the NUPIC underground indies, been featured as part of the Slam Legends Showcase, and has been Haiku Deathmatch Champion. She's been published in *PANK* and *Los Angeles Review of Books* as well as peer-reviewed journals for her research on the healing effects of writing.

In real life—as a psychologist, mother, wife, friend, mentor, and freelance evangelist—Cheryl spends her time encouraging people to find their real best self and to stick by that person, no matter what.